Rights of
the Accused

CRIME, JUSTICE, AND PUNISHMENT

Rights of the Accused

Andrea Campbell

Austin Sarat, GENERAL EDITOR

CHELSEA HOUSE PUBLISHERS
Philadelphia

Frontispiece: The Constitution of the United States guarantees certain rights to every citizen, including those accused of crime.

Chelsea House Publishers

Editor in Chief Stephen Reginald
Production Manager Pamela Loos
Art Director Sara Davis
Director of Photography Judy L. Hasday
Managing Editor James D. Gallagher
Senior Production Editor J. Christopher Higgins

Staff for RIGHTS OF THE ACCUSED

Associate Art Director Takeshi Takahashi
Designer Keith Trego
Picture Researcher Marty Levick
Cover Designer Keith Trego

First Printing

1 3 5 7 9 8 6 4 2

The Chelsea House World Wide Web address is
http://www.chelseahouse.com

Library of Congress Cataloging-in-Publication Data

Campbell, Andrea.
Rights of the Accused / Andrea Campbell.
    p. cm. — (Crime, justice, and punishment)
Includes bibliographical references and index.
Summary: Explains how and why the Fourth, Fifth, and Sixth Amendments to the Constitution protect the rights of those accused of a crime.

ISBN 0-7910-4303-7 (hc)

1. Due process of law—United States—Juvenile literature.
2. Fair trial—United States—Juvenile literature. [1. Due process of law. 2. Fair trial.] I. Title. II. Series.
KF4765.Z9 C36 2000
347.73'5—dc21   00-024992

Contents

CRIME, JUSTICE, AND PUNISHMENT

Fears and Fascinations:

An Introduction to Crime, Justice, and Punishment

By Austin Sarat

We live with crime and images of crime all around us. Crime evokes in most of us a deep aversion, a feeling of profound vulnerability, but it also evokes an equally deep fascination. Today, in major American cities the fear of crime is a major fact of life, some would say a disproportionate response to the realities of crime. Yet the fear of crime is real, palpable in the quickened steps and furtive glances of people walking down darkened streets. At the same time, we eagerly follow crime stories on television and in movies. We watch with a "who done it" curiosity, eager to see the illicit deed done, the investigation undertaken, the miscreant brought to justice and given his just deserts. On the streets the presence of crime is a reminder of our own vulnerability and the precariousness of our taken-for-granted rights and freedoms. On television and in the movies the crime story gives us a chance to probe our own darker motives, to ask "Is there a criminal within?" as well as to feel the collective satisfaction of seeing justice done.

Fear and fascination, these two poles of our engagement with crime, are, of course, only part of the story. Crime is, after all, a major social and legal problem, not just an issue of our individual psychology. Politicians today use our fear of, and fascination with, crime for political advantage. How we respond to crime, as well as to the political uses of the crime issue, tells us a lot about who we are as a people as well as what we value and what we tolerate. Is our response compassionate or severe? Do we seek to understand or to punish, to enact an angry vengeance or to rehabilitate and welcome the criminal back into our midst? The CRIME, JUSTICE, AND PUNISHMENT series is designed to explore these themes, to ask why we are fearful and fascinated, to probe the meanings and motivations of crimes and criminals and of our responses to them, and, finally, to ask what we can learn about ourselves and the society in which we live by examining our responses to crime.

Crime is always a challenge to the prevailing normative order and a test of the values and commitments of law-abiding people. It is sometimes a Raskolnikov-like act of defiance, an assertion of the unwillingness of some to live according to the rules of conduct laid out by organized society. In this sense, crime marks the limits of the law and reminds us of law's all-too-regular failures. Yet sometimes there is more desperation than defiance in criminal acts; sometimes they signal a deep pathology or need in the criminal. To confront crime is thus also to come face-to-face with the reality of social difference, of class privilege and extreme deprivation, of race and racism, of children neglected, abandoned, or abused whose response is to enact on others what they have experienced themselves. And occasionally crime, or what is labeled a criminal act, represents a call for justice, an appeal to a higher moral order against the inadequacies of existing law.

Figuring out the meaning of crime and the motivations of criminals and whether crime arises from defiance, desperation, or the appeal for justice is never an easy task. The motivations and meanings of crime are as varied as are the persons who engage in criminal conduct. They are as mysterious as any of the mysteries of the human soul. Yet the desire to know the secrets of crime and the criminal is a strong one, for in that knowledge may lie one step on the road to protection, if not an assurance of one's own personal safety. Nonetheless, as strong as that desire may be, there is no available technology that can allow us to know the whys of crime with much confidence, let alone a scientific certainty. We can, however, capture something about crime by studying the defiance, desperation, and quest for justice that may be associated with it. Books in the CRIME, JUSTICE, AND PUNISHMENT series will take up that challenge. They tell stories of crime and criminals, some famous, most not, some glamorous and exciting, most mundane and commonplace.

This series will, in addition, take a sober look at American criminal justice, at the procedures through which we investigate crimes and identify criminals, at the institutions in which innocence or guilt is determined. In these procedures and institutions we confront the thrill of the chase as well as the challenge of protecting the rights of those who defy our laws. It is through the efficiency and dedication of law enforcement that we might capture the criminal; it is in the rare instances of their corruption or brutality that we feel perhaps our deepest betrayal. Police, prosecutors, defense lawyers, judges, and jurors administer criminal justice and in their daily actions give substance to the guarantees of the Bill of Rights. What is an adversarial system of justice? How does it work? Why do we have it? Books in the CRIME, JUSTICE, AND PUNISHMENT series will examine the thrill of the chase as we seek to capture the criminal. They will also reveal the drama and majesty of the criminal trial as well as the day-to-day reality of a criminal justice system in which trials are the exception and negotiated pleas of guilty are the rule.

When the trial is over or the plea has been entered, when we have separated the innocent from the guilty, the moment of punishment has arrived. The injunction to punish the guilty, to respond to pain inflicted by inflicting pain, is as old as civilization itself. "An eye for an eye and a tooth for a tooth" is a biblical reminder that punishment must measure pain for pain. But our response to the criminal must be better than and different from the crime itself. The biblical admonition, along with the constitutional prohibition of "cruel and unusual punishment," signals that we seek to punish justly and to be just not only in the determination of who can and should be punished, but in how we punish as well. But neither reminder tells us what to do with the wrongdoer. Do we rape the rapist, or burn the home of the arsonist? Surely justice and decency say no. But, if not, then how can and should we punish? In a world in which punishment is neither identical to the crime nor an automatic response to it, choices must be made and we must make them. Books in the CRIME, JUSTICE, AND PUNISHMENT series will examine those choices and the practices, and politics, of punishment. How do we punish and why do we punish as we do? What can we learn about the rationality and appropriateness of today's responses to crime by examining our past and its responses? What works? Is there, and can there be, a just measure of pain?

CRIME, JUSTICE, AND PUNISHMENT brings together books on some of the great themes of human social life. The books in this series capture our fear and fascination with crime and examine our responses to it. They remind us of the deadly seriousness of these subjects. They bring together themes in law, literature, and popular culture to challenge us to think again, to think anew, about subjects that go to the heart of who we are and how we can and will live together.

*   *   *   *   *

There is probably no more engaging and controversial subject in the area of crime, justice, and punishment than the rights of the accused. Here searches and seizures, compelled confessions, the right to counsel, and other issues provide the grist for fascinating arguments as well as gripping episodes of films and television programs. What some see as essential to the meaning of American constitutionalism and to the protection of rights, others see as mere technicalities. Here the question of the balance between society's desire for security and our concern to protect the rights even of persons accused of crime is at the forefront.

This book is a timely and important addition to the literature on the rights of the accused. It addresses key debates and provides an historical context for contemporary debates. Its chapters tell the story behind key provisions of the Bill of Rights—the Fourth, Fifth, and Sixth Amendments—and, through fascinating case studies, draw us into what is most engaging about the subject of the rights of the accused. Throughout it shows how and why rights change and that citizens need to be vigilant and active in debating what the rights of the accused should be and in protecting our constitutional rights.

WHY DO THE ACCUSED NEED PROTECTION?

When Gary Gauger awoke one morning in 1993 to find his parents lying dead in a pool of blood, the 40-year-old farmer's reaction was to call 911.

McHenry County sheriffs quickly arrived at the family's Richmond, Illinois, farmhouse to investigate the crime scene. They found no sign of forced entry and no sign of robbers. In fact, money and valuable items had been left behind by the killer. Also, there was no sign of struggle. Morrie and Ruth Gauger's throats had been slashed in the kitchen, less than 30 feet away from where Gary had been sleeping, yet he had not woken.

For these reasons police suspected Gary Gauger may have committed the crime. His conduct, investi-

Gary Gauger, an Illinois farmer, was wrongfully convicted of murdering his parents. He spent several years on death row until his conviction was overturned. When the rights of the accused are ignored by police, prosecutors, and the courts, as in the Gauger case, the innocent may suffer instead of the guilty.

gators thought, was even more suspicious. Police expected him to be grief-stricken at the brutal murder of his parents, but he quietly tended his tomato plants while the sheriffs conducted their investigation. Based on this reaction, Gauger was an obvious suspect.

The police took him to their headquarters for questioning. Their interrogation lasted 18 hours; Gauger was not allowed to eat or sleep, he could not call a lawyer, and the proceedings were not recorded.

During the questioning the police asked Gauger to describe how he might—hypothetically—slash his parents' throats. Trying to be helpful, Gauger complied. The police also told the farmer that they had found his bloody fingerprints on the weapon used to commit the murders—a fact that was untrue.

"My parents had just been murdered and these were the good guys," Gauger said later. "I know it sounds naive now, but when they told me they wouldn't lie to me, I believed them."

The pressure of the nonstop interrogation took a toll on the quiet, ex-hippie farmer. Gauger smoked marijuana and had at one time been a heavy drinker. In the past he had experienced blackouts, periods during which he could not recall his actions. It was possible, an exhausted Gauger told police, that he had blacked out and killed his parents.

Although he then explained that he had not been drinking, and repeatedly said that he did not think he had committed the crime, the McHenry County sheriffs were convinced. Even though a 10-day search of the property turned up no evidence that linked Gauger to the crime, he was arrested and charged with the murder of his parents.

At trial Gauger was represented by attorneys who were inexperienced at defending a capital murder case. The prosecutor painted Gauger as a crazy man. The judge rolled his eyes at one point during the farmer's testimony, and when the defense attorneys protested, he simply turned his back on the accused man. It took just three hours for the jury to reach a guilty verdict. Afterward the jury foreman called Gauger "nutty as a fruitcake." Gary Gauger was sentenced to die by lethal injection and placed on Illinois's death row.

The Constitution of the United States, a document that sets out the basic laws of our nation and the powers of government, provides certain rights to all citizens. Under the Constitution, people accused of a crime are guaranteed certain protections. One of these is the right to due process of the law, which means that all those accused of a crime will go through the same steps in the legal process and that laws will apply to all equally. Others include the right to legal counsel, the right not to be unreasonably searched, the right to confront witnesses and accusers in court, and the right against self-incrimination.

These rights have been set forth in the Bill of Rights, a term given to the first 10 amendments to the Constitution. The Fourth, Fifth, and Sixth Amendments are directly aimed at protecting individuals' rights when they are subject to a criminal investigation and trial. The Eighth Amendment guarantees that those convicted of crimes will not be subject to "excessive" fines or "cruel and unusual punishment."

The Constitution provides a framework for our legal system. However, in the more than 200 years since its passage, many specific laws have been passed. The Supreme Court, our nation's highest judicial body, is often called upon to rule on important cases related to these laws. When the Supreme Court reaches a majority decision and rules on a case, its rule becomes precedent that must be honored by all lower courts. The Supreme Court's influence helps to shape the everyday operations of the police, corrections departments, and trial courts. Supreme Court decisions establish the procedures that must be followed to ensure all those accused of crimes receive due process of the law.

The story of Gary Gauger illustrates how the criminal justice system can break down if individual rights are not protected. Interrogating Gauger without allowing him to have a lawyer present violated the protections guaranteed by the Fifth Amendment, which the Supreme Court established in the landmark case *Miranda v. Arizona* (1966). Police or prosecutors must explain the accused's rights before beginning an investigation and allow his or her attorney to be present during questioning. Interrogators are not allowed to physically harm the accused to force him or her to confess; they are also prohibited from trying to psychologically trick or intimidate the accused into confessing guilt.

Gary Gauger was fortunate. After his sentencing Gary's twin sister, Ginger, contacted a Northwestern University law school professor named Lawrence C. Marshall, who had made something of a career defending wrongly accused death row inmates. Marshall took the case. Pointing out how Gauger's rights had been violated, and the circumstantial evidence prosecutors had used to convict the farmer, Marshall won Gauger's freedom in 1996. "The evidence against Gauger was woefully weak, but [his original] lawyers . . . failed to prove that his supposed confession did not come close to matching the facts of the crime and utterly failed to put on any real defense at the sentencing stage of the case," the attorney later wrote in the *Chicago Tribune*.

In the meantime, FBI agents listening in on a wiretap heard members of the Outlaws, a motorcycle gang, discussing the murders of Morrie and Ruth Gauger. In 1997, Randall "Madman" Miller and James "Preacher" Schneider were arrested and charged with killing the Gaugers and stealing $15, which they had used to buy breakfast.

The Constitution provides a framework for the government of the United States, and offers equal protection to all citizens. The U.S. Constitution is the supreme law of the land; no other law, state statute, or executive order can supercede it.

❦   ❦   ❦

The protections granted under the Constitution are often debated as they are applied to specific cases. Today's society is filled with violent crime: although the incidence of crimes like homicide, rape, robbery, and assault has fallen in general, more than 80 percent of Americans will experience some sort of violent crime in their lifetime. More than ever, citizens want to feel safe. As a result, they are willing to give police great authority to handle crime—but at the same time most Americans would be outraged if they were asked to give up the protections offered under the Bill of Rights. This creates a tug-of-war between the citizens' desire for security versus their need for Constitutional protection. The ongoing debate between the two sides will continue as long as opinions change regarding the level of freedom that should be sacrificed to preserve the social order.

Mary Broderick, who is with the National Legal Aid and Defense Association, says that average citizens believe *their* rights are the most important to protect—not the criminal's. They believe that the justice system favors the criminal too much. "In fact," she says, "the [debates regarding] rights of the accused are a symptom of a society myth—that most persons arrested for a crime are convicted." As a result, because many citizens are convinced that the accused person is nearly always guilty, sometimes the emphasis of the prosecution is put on conviction rather than justice. To observers the prosecutor may seem to be the "good guy," while the defense attorney is on the criminal's side.

In theory, of course, most of us would support the idea that the same procedures ought to be followed for everyone accused of a crime, no matter who he or she is. But in reality, society is not always so generous. Few of us think twice about our procedural rights, and we almost never realize how important they are until the accusing finger is pointed at us. We forget that the

defense attorney protects our rights just as much as the prosecutor does.

In fact, most of the time we take our constitutional rights for granted. Early Americans, however, did not come up with the Bill of Rights accidentally or by coincidence; each amendment was carefully and thoughtfully hammered out in reaction to real-life violations of citizens' rights by the British Empire. The new government wanted to prevent similar abuses of the law.

As we gain a historical perspective on the rights of the accused, perhaps we will see more clearly why these rights are so essential to our society.

In a society awash in violence, many people are willing to give police broad authority to handle crime. However, this authority must be tempered with the understanding that the accused are entitled to certain rights.

THE HISTORY BEHIND OUR RIGHTS

Discontented farmers seize the Massachusetts Court House during the 1786 uprising led by Daniel Shays. Known as Shays's Rebellion, the revolt spurred the 13 fledgling states to convene the Constitutional Convention in Philadelphia in 1787. There, a new federal constitution was drafted to replace the old Articles of Confederation that had bound the states since 1781.

On a fall day in 1786 in the western part of Massachusetts, Daniel Shays led a group of farmers in an armed rebellion against the state government. The farmers were angry because the government had taxed them heavily—and then, when they were unable to keep up with their taxes, the state had seized their land and possessions; some of them had even been imprisoned. The farmers reasoned that their individual freedoms had been threatened—after all, hadn't they recently fought for independence from England over this very issue of unfair taxation?—while the state government felt equally as strongly that the state's peace and security were threatened by Shays's rebels. Massachusetts asked the new American Congress for aid in putting down the rebellion, but Congress could do little to help; the central government lacked money and troops, and consequently could do next to nothing to maintain order and security. Massachusetts was eventually able to raise the funds from its wealthiest citizens to hire troops, and the rebellion ended in February 1787 with the capture or flight of the rebel leaders (who were later pardoned).

However, news of Shays's Rebellion spread through the 13 states. Many citizens in the new nation were worried. If this could happen in Massachusetts, they realized, then it could happen again somewhere else. Their young federal government had no power to protect the citizens' security—and a nation could not function and grow without that basic stability and safety.

Prompted by these fears, all the states except Rhode Island sent delegates to attend a convention in Philadelphia in the spring of 1787. After four long months of discussion these delegates eventually wrote what is now our Constitution, the document that spells out our legal system. George Washington, the convention's president, was the first to sign.

As these early Americans shaped the laws that still govern our nation today, they were influenced by the legal system of their mother country, England. English law had been developed over the centuries, a mishmash of tribal rules, Roman laws, British customs, and historical edicts made by judges in response to particular situations. This legal system was called English common law—"common" because when William the Conqueror began his rule of England in 1066, he decreed that the entire land would have these laws in common in one consolidated system. It was a collection of legal decisions handed down from generation to generation, and included within this ancient legal system were laws that balanced the rights of the accused against English society's need for security.

We can find elements of English common law in the Constitution. However, early Americans were also influenced by the fact that they had rebelled against the mother country. From their perspective the English government's need for stability had trespassed on their individual rights. As a result, when the Constitution

A draft of the Bill of Rights, a list of amendments to the Constitution. These amendments lay out the basic rights of citizens, with the Fourth, Fifth, and Sixth Amendments primarily concerned with the rights of persons accused of crime. This draft includes 12 amendments; in 1791 the states ratified 10 of them.

was written, its authors included safeguards against a government that could steal too much of an individual's freedom. They did not want a repeat performance of the unjust government they had fought so hard to escape. That is why the Constitution's authors were careful to work out compromises between state security on one hand and individual freedom on the other.

Once the Constitution was written, its authors next had to convince the states to ratify, or approve, the document. This was not an easy task. Many Americans were reluctant to create a powerful central government—and they certainly did not want one that might trample on their individual rights. In their minds the memory of all the British had done to suppress their fight for independence was still too fresh. These people wanted to include in the Constitution a list of specific guarantees of freedom that would define and protect the individual's rights.

Finally eight states did ratify the Constitution. One more of the thirteen states was needed to approve it if the Constitution was to be adopted by the new nation. Two of the states that were holding out were New York and Virginia; both were reluctant to ratify the Constitution unless a list of amendments that spelled out individual freedoms was included. In Virginia, James Madison promised to push for a bill of rights to be amended to the Constitution if he was elected to the new Congress.

Eventually all 13 of the states did ratify the Constitution, but many of them insisted that a bill of rights had to be added to the original document. Madison, who had won his election to the House of Representatives, kept his campaign promise and proposed constitutional amendments that would protect people's individual rights. The House agreed to 17 amendments; the Senate cut the list to 14; and in September 1789 the House and Senate agreed on 12 amendments. The states ratified 10 of these—the Bill of Rights.

Included in the Bill of Rights are guarantees that specifically protect the rights of someone who has been accused of a crime. For example, the Fourth Amendment guarantees the right against unreasonable search and seizure. This was a response to the English practice of issuing general warrants, which allowed the government and its agents to search anywhere, anytime, and for any reason "as long as the King lives." The men who fought for freedom from Great Britain felt that this statute had been abused by the English, especially by the troops that had been quartered in colonial America before the Revolution.

The Fifth Amendment works together with the Fourth to protect a suspect's rights. It guarantees that the accused cannot be forced to confess, stipulates the right against self-incrimination, and provides that all those accused of serious crimes will have their cases reviewed by a special jury.

Other amendments providing rights to the accused include the Sixth Amendment, which ensures the suspect's right to be represented by legal counsel and the right to a trial by his or her peers. This helps to guarantee that the poor will not be underrepresented and thereby made victims of the courts. The Seventh Amendment extends the right of a jury trial to civil lawsuits as well as criminal cases. It also protects individuals from the federal government reopening a state trial and overturning the jury's decision. And the Eighth Amendment, as previously noted, protects persons convicted of a crime from excessive fines or punishments.

All these amendments that define the rights of the accused have a certain fluidity, depending on how the Supreme Court justices interpret them. The nine justices of the Supreme Court decide the most difficult cases, setting precedents for future application of laws throughout the country.

However, throughout much of America's history

Freed African Americans line up to vote in the South after the Civil War. The Fourteenth Amendment, passed in 1868, gave former slaves and all others born or naturalized in the United States the same rights of citizenship. It also provided that the state or federal governments could not "deprive any person of life, liberty, or property, without due process of law; nor deny to any person within its jurisdiction the equal protection of the laws."

only 10 percent of criminal defendants tried in this country were tried in federal court. The rest were tried in state courts, and often the privileges provided by the Bill of Rights were superseded by state laws. As a result, until the 20th century criminal defendants did not always receive the protections they were entitled to under the Constitution.

In 1868 the Fourteenth Amendment was added to the Constitution. This amendment was passed after the Civil War to give former slaves official status as citizens of the United States, but it also stated clearly that state laws could not take away any of the rights provided by the Constitution. "No state shall make or enforce any law which shall abridge the privileges or immunities of citizens of the United States; nor shall any State deprive any person of life, liberty, or property, without due process of law; nor deny to any person within its jurisdiction the equal protection of the laws," the Fourteenth Amendment states.

There was no question at the time that the amendment applied to state governments. It was written to tie national and state laws together, and ensure that all citizens would receive the same protections under the law. Still, more than six decades passed before the Fourteenth Amendment's due process clause was interpreted by the Supreme Court to mean that no state could infringe on the rights of the accused that are guaranteed by the Bill of Rights.

In the tug-of-war between a society's need for both security and individual freedom, the Bill of Rights continues to protect the individual against governmental interference. The Fourth, Fifth, and Sixth Amendments, in particular, guarantee the rights of the accused.

THE FOURTH AMENDMENT: SEARCH AND SEIZURE

> *The right of the people to be secure in their persons, houses, papers, and effects, against unreasonable searches and seizures, shall not be violated, and no Warrants shall issue, but upon probable cause, supported by Oath or affirmation, and particularly describing the place to be searched, and the persons or things to be seized.*

O n May 20, 1957, someone set off a bomb that demolished the front porch and wall of a home owned by Don King of Cleveland, Ohio. Three days after the bombing, three Cleveland policemen, acting on a phone tip, drove to the home of a woman named Dollree Mapp. The three plain-clothesmen had been told that a suspect named Virgil Ogiltree was at Mapp's house. When they arrived, his car was parked outside.

The officers waited to apprehend Ogiltree when he left the house, but he never came out. Becoming

A policeman frisks a criminal suspect. The Fourth Amendment, and its interpretation by the Supreme Court over the years, sets guidelines for police searches.

One of the things that angered the American colonists before the start of the Revolution was the "writs of assistance" issued by King George III of England. These allowed British troops to enter and search colonists' homes and property at any time.

impatient, the policemen knocked on Mapp's door to make inquiries. Ms. Mapp answered but refused to let them inside, telling the policemen that she would not allow them to search without a warrant, nor would she open the door without first calling her lawyer. The men retreated, but they kept the house under surveillance and radioed another officer to obtain a warrant.

Later, a half-dozen uniformed men came back and claimed they had a warrant. Mapp again refused to open the door, so the officers entered the residence by breaking a pane of glass, unlatching the door, and charging up to Mapp's second-floor apartment. She met them on the landing. "Where's the warrant?" she demanded. One of the officers, Sergeant Carl Delau, held up a piece of paper, which Mapp grabbed and stuffed under her turtleneck. Once the officers had handcuffed her, they snatched back the paper from inside her shirt. They then searched the residence and confiscated some obscene materials—pencil sketches of nude models and four books—as well as paraphernalia used for illegal betting. Ogiltree was not found.

Dollree Mapp was arrested and charged with possession of gambling equipment and obscene materials. The latter offense was listed as a felony under a newly amended state statute against pornography. By the time Mapp was brought to trial in September 1958, the search warrant police had produced before their search had disappeared. (Twenty years later Delau would admit that his trial testimony had been untrue; in fact, his lieutenant had only obtained an affidavit, a document spelling out the reasons for wanting a warrant.)

Mapp was found guilty on the obscenity charge based on the evidence collected during the police search. She was sentenced to one to seven years in the Ohio State Reformatory for Women. When she appealed, the Ohio Supreme Court upheld the lower court's ruling, stating that her conviction was valid even though it was "based primarily upon the introduction of lewd and lascivious books and pictures unlawfully seized during an unlawful search of [the] defendant's home."

Eventually the Mapp case reached the U.S. Supreme Court, which consented to review her appeal because the Fourth Amendment protects the right of citizens against unreasonable searches and seizures.

The Fourth Amendment determines how evidence can be gathered and seized for the courts. The dramas depicted on television and in movies sometimes portray law enforcement officials crashing into residences, pushing people around, and secretly gathering evidence that can be used later to prove their case. In real life, however, citizens are protected from these scenarios by the Fourth Amendment. According to this amendment, all Americans have the right to be "secure in their persons, houses, papers, and effects, against unreasonable searches and seizures." In effect, this means that the police must go before a judge or magistrate and obtain a warrant that specifically describes the place to be searched and the article to be seized. In order for the warrant to be granted, the police must show "probable cause"; in other words, they must convince a court that there is good reason to suspect that evidence of a crime will be found during a search.

The authors of the Bill of Rights were all too aware of the need for this amendment. In the years before the Revolutionary War, King George III of England issued "writs of assistance" to his agents; these writs gave them authority to search for smuggled goods wherever and whenever they wanted. One early Revolutionary leader declared that the writs of assistance were "the worst instrument of arbitrary power," because they put "the liberty of every man in the hands of every officer."

Until the 20th century, though, the Fourth Amendment was not consistently enforced. If police invaded a person's home illegally, that person's only option was to file a lawsuit against the police. Court battles were expensive, and most juries tended to sympathize with law enforcement officials; as a result, few victims of unjustified searches ever brought suit against the police.

In 1914, however, in a court case called *Weeks v. United States*, the Supreme Court issued what came to be called the exclusionary rule. This ruling dictated that illegally obtained evidence had to be excluded from (or kept out of) criminal trials in federal courts. Unfortunately for those accused of a crime, this did not apply uniformly to state courts until the Supreme Court's 1961 decision in *Mapp v. Ohio*. This case set the precedent to determine what exactly an "unreasonable search and seizure" is, in a state criminal trial as well as a federal one.

The Court ruled in the *Mapp* case that the police had conducted an illegal search and seizure. Not only had police violated Mapp's right to privacy, but they had asked for a warrant to search the premises for a bombing suspect, not for the items that were eventually used as evidence to prosecute Mapp.

Basic Elements Required for an Arrest

Basis of Knowledge:	The information that must be included in an affidavit: who, what, when, where, and why
Affidavit:	An affidavit based on an informant's tip must set forth sufficient underlying circumstances to permit a neutral and detached magistrate to understand how the informant reached his or her conclusion
Judge:	Probable cause is required for a judge's signature.
Warrant:	Spells out facts and needs
Evidence:	Supports police belief that the accused person has committed a crime

Police officers make an arrest during a drug bust. To enter a suspect's home, police must first convince a judge that they have probable cause to suspect illegal activities are going on there, and must obtain a search warrant that spells out specifically what the police are looking for.

This decision firmly established that a search warrant does not mean a suspect completely forfeits his or her right to privacy. If a policeman receives a warrant to search a suspect's garage for a stolen car, the officer may only look for evidence in the garage and may only look for evidence that is related to the case. Even if the policeman conducting the search happens to find other evidence in the suspect's home, it would be excluded from any trial unless the warrant specifically allowed police to look for that evidence in that place.

A law enforcement official speaks with suspects in a subway tunnel. There is a difference between a "stop" and an "arrest": police are permitted to detain a person briefly to question him or her about suspected criminal activity.

The law has been modified since the *Mapp* ruling. Now, incidental evidence that is uncovered by police conducting a lawful search can be included in trials, as long as the search can be shown by the police to be a good-faith effort to conform with the Fourth Amendment. In 1984 the Supreme Court further modified the exclusionary rule with an exception called inevitable discovery, meaning that any evidence of criminal activity that is discovered in violation of a defendant's Fourth Amendment rights can still be used in a trial, as long as the prosecution can prove that the evidence would have been discovered in the course of a lawful search.

However, the exclusionary rule has also been extended to provide further rights for the accused as well. In the early 1960s, six federal narcotics agents illegally broke into a laundry because they suspected the owner of selling drugs. Once in, they chased the owner,

James Wah Toy, into the living quarters at the back of his shop, where his wife and child were sleeping. There they arrested and handcuffed him. Toy then told agents that another man, John "Johnny" Yee, had been selling narcotics. The agents immediately went to Yee, who surrendered heroin to them and implicated Toy and another man, Wong Sun. In the case *Wong Sun v. United States* (1963), a five-to-four Supreme Court majority held that Toy's declarations after being hand-cuffed in his bedroom and also the narcotics taken from Yee, to which Toy's declarations had led the police, had to be excluded. Both were the result of the agents' unlawful entry into Toy's bedroom. This ruling illus-trates an extension of the exclusionary rule that is referred to as the "fruit of the poisonous tree." This concept prohibits the admission of evidence obtained as a result of an illegally or initially tainted admission, confession, or search.

This is a very important right for someone accused of crime. However, many law enforcement officials are not fond of the exclusionary rule or its extensions. They maintain that the chief purpose of the exclusionary rule is to punish police trying to do their job of enforcing the law. The real question, though, is not whether good-faith mistakes on the part of the police are treated too harshly, but whether the justice system provides citizens feelings of security.

The rules concerning search and seizure are con-stantly being tested. However, contrary to popular belief, the number of criminals freed by the exclusion-ary rule each year is very small. In fact, less than 1 per-cent of federal criminal cases have been dropped because of searches violating the Fourth Amendment.

Many times we like to think in terms of black and white, good and bad, but the enforcement of the Fourth Amendment is often unclear and complicated. A prob-lem can arise when a third party becomes involved. The Supreme Court's 1990 decision in *Illinois v.*

Rodriguez is an example of how third-party consent to searches can become a legal tangle.

On July 26, 1985, Chicago police were summoned to the residence of Dorothy Jackson on South Wolcott Street. Jackson's daughter, Gail Fischer, met the officers there and told them she had been assaulted by Edward Rodriguez earlier that day in an apartment on South California Street. Fischer, who showed signs of a severe beating, told the policemen that Rodriguez was asleep, and offered to take the police to the apartment and unlock the door with her key so they could arrest him. In their report the officers noted that Fischer referred to the place as "our apartment" and said she had clothes and furniture there. Although she had obviously lived with Rodriguez in the past, however, the police were uncertain whether she was living with him at the time of the search.

Police drove to South California Street accompanied by Fischer. They did not obtain an arrest warrant for Rodriguez or seek a search warrant for the apartment. Once they arrived, Fischer unlocked the door for police and gave them permission to enter. In the living room, the policemen observed drug paraphernalia in plain view, as well as containers filled with white powder, which they assumed was cocaine. Rodriguez was asleep in the bedroom, and similar containers of powder were visible nearby in open attaché cases. The officers arrested him and seized the drugs and related goods. He was charged with possession of a controlled substance with intent to deliver.

Rodriguez's lawyer moved to suppress all evidence seized, claiming that Fischer had vacated the apartment several weeks earlier and had no authority to allow the policemen to enter. A judge on the Circuit Court of Cook County granted this motion, noting that Fischer did not have common authority over the apartment. She was an "infrequent visitor," her name was not on the lease, she did not contribute to the rent, she was not allowed to invite others into the apartment, and she did not have access to it when Rodriguez was away. The circuit court also rejected the state's contention that even if Fischer did not have common authority over the premises, there was no Fourth Amendment violation if the police reasonably believed at the time that Fischer did have standing. An Illinois appellate court upheld this decision.

The U.S. Supreme Court reversed the judgment of the Illinois court. The Court's official opinion explained this decision: "Because many situations which confront officers in the course of executing their duties are more or less ambiguous, room must be allowed for some mistakes on their part. But the mistakes must be those of reasonable men, acting on facts leading sensibly to their conclusions of probability." The Court found that the Constitution is no more violated when officers enter without a warrant because they reasonably (though erroneously) believe that the person who has consented to their entry is a resident of the premises, than it is violated when they enter without a warrant because they reasonably (though erroneously) believe they are in pursuit of a violent felon who is about to escape.

The next logical question that arises about home arrest is whether the police are required to announce their presence. This is also referred to as the "no knock rule." Under federal statutes and many state laws, police officers must announce their "authority and purpose" before using force to enter a home to make an arrest. Generally, failure to make such a pronouncement renders the arrest unlawful, although most jurisdictions recognize exceptions to this requirement. Some of these exceptions include the officer's reasonable belief that the announcement would endanger the officer or others, such as children in trouble, or that it might prompt a suspect's escape, or permit the destruction of evidence.

In 1988, the Supreme Court went a step further in hammering out the balance between the rights of the accused and the protection of public safety. In *California v. Greenwood* the Court ruled that evidence police had found in Greenwood's trash was admissible in court and could be used to convict him of selling and using drugs. In other words, individuals cannot have an expectation of privacy based on materials that they make publicly available.

The Fourth Amendment also provides the principles for a constitutional arrest. Placing a person under arrest establishes a seizure of the body, since authorities are in effect taking away the person's freedom to leave. Defense attorneys agree that there is a big difference as to how suspects should be treated, what their rights are, and what is required of them, depending on whether they are under arrest or not. Michael Saeger, author of the book *Defend Yourself Against Criminal Charges*, says the easiest way for people to know if they're being detained is to inquire: "Am I under arrest?" He suggests that until suspects know this, there is no way to determine if they can come and go, and no way to decide if they must abide by the instructions given by the police.

Police have specific protocol they must adhere to in order to meet their objective for a constitutional arrest. First of all, an arrest, with or without a warrant, needs to meet the requirement of probable cause. Probable cause means that the facts and circumstances the officer believes to be true at the time of arrest must be based on reasonably trustworthy information.

The next step in the process is to secure a warrant (if a warrant is necessary). A warrant for arrest is valid only if it is based on a complaint or a document called an affidavit, which sets forth certain facts showing both the commission of an offense and the accuser's responsibility attached to it. Obtaining that warrant follows certain constitutional standards too; a judge will only sign it if the probable cause is spelled out in writing. At least that's the way the system should operate. Realistically, the potential for a problem always exists.

Literally thousands of variations on the search-and-seizure issue wind up in appellate court. These cases serve to carve out the process in more detail. For instance, the issue of how to approach and search a person suspected of a potential crime was defined through a specific case, *Terry v. Ohio* (1968).

At about 2:30 in the afternoon one day in October 1963, a Cleveland plainclothes detective, Officer Martin McFadden, observed several men standing on a street corner in the downtown area. One of the suspects walked up Huron Road, peered into a store, walked on and then started back, looked into the store again, and then conferred with his companions. Another suspect followed the same procedure, and they went through this process some 12 times, as if they were casing the store prior to a robbery. McFadden became suspicious of their behavior. Then a member of the group went up the street, and after about 10 minutes the others followed him. McFadden followed too.

He confronted the men as they were talking and identified himself, then asked for the suspects' names. The men responded with mumbles. Fearing the men might be armed, the officer spun a man named Terry around and patted his breast pocket. He felt a pistol, which he then removed. A frisk of Terry's first companion revealed another weapon, but the third man was unarmed and he was not searched any further.

Terry was charged with possessing a concealed weapon. Later his lawyer moved to have the weapon suppressed as evidence. The motion was denied by a trial judge, the Ohio Court of Appeals confirmed it, and the state supreme court dismissed Terry's appeal.

This case was eventually heard by the Supreme Court, which upheld the lower court rulings. The Supreme Court ruled that in circumstances where dangerous situations are unfolding on city streets, the police need to have an escalating set of flexible responses, graduating in intensity according to the amount of information they possess. The judges agreed that a distinction should be made between a "stop" and an "arrest," and between a "frisk" and a "search." They decided police should be allowed to stop a person and detain him or her briefly for questioning on suspicion that he or she may be connected to a criminal activity. If police are also suspicious the person may be armed, they should be able to frisk for weapons. If the stop and frisk lead to probable cause that the suspect may have committed a crime, police should then be empowered to make a formal arrest, which would allow for a full search. The judges felt that this definition of procedure was justified in the interest of effective law enforcement, even if it amounted to a "minor inconvenience and petty indignity" being imposed on a citizen.

Making an arrest without a warrant is possible, but the circumstances must meet certain specifications. If the police have reasonable grounds to believe that a felony has been committed, and if they have a particular person in mind, an arrest can be made. If a misdemeanor is committed in the presence of a law enforcement officer, that would also be grounds for a valid arrest. There are other situations for warrantless arrests as well, as the case *United States v. Watson* (1976) demonstrates.

In this case a reliable informant named Awad

"Stop" or "Arrest"?

The Arkansas Law Enforcement Training Academy has a chart that spells out the difference between a stop and an arrest:

	STOP	ARREST
Justification:	Reasonable suspicion	Probable cause
Search:	Possibly a "pat down"	Complete body search
Record:	Minimal	Fingerprints, photographs, and booking
Intent of Officer:	To resolve ambiguous situation	To make a formal charge

Khoury told a postal inspector that he had supplied a man named Watson with a stolen credit card. He had agreed to turn over additional cards at their next meeting, which was scheduled to take place at a restaurant location a few days later. As decided ahead of time, Khoury signaled the inspector when Watson had the cards, at which point the postal inspector arrested Watson without a warrant, as he was authorized to do under postal regulations.

The court of appeals held the arrest unconstitutional because the inspector had failed to secure a warrant, even though he admitted to having had time to do so. This error in judgment had bearing on the court's additional ruling that Watson's consent to a search of his car was not voluntary.

Eventually, however, the Supreme Court reversed the appellate court's decision on the grounds that each case should be considered under historical guidelines— if the felony was committed in the presence of law enforcement or if there were reasonable grounds to arrest. Therefore, the Court ruled the arrest was legal, stating that to permit felony arrests only with a warrant or in exigent circumstances (those requiring immediate action) could severely hamper effective law enforcement's capabilities.

Four years earlier, the Supreme Court had established that law enforcement officials cannot be so constrained by protocol that they cannot respond to situations in which crime is occurring. In the Court's decision in *Adams v. Williams* (1972), Justice William Rehnquist wrote:

> [The] Fourth Amendment does not require a policeman who lacks the precise level of information necessary for probable cause to arrest to simply shrug his shoulders and allow a crime to occur or a criminal to escape. On the contrary, *Terry v. Ohio* recognizes that it may be the essence of good police work to adopt an intermediate response. . . . A brief stop of a suspicious individual, in

Although arrests can be made without a warrant, the legal system entitles a suspect to receive a probable-cause hearing within 48 hours of his or her arrest.

order to determine his identity or to maintain the status quo momentarily, while obtaining more information, may be the most reasonable in light of the facts known to the officer at the time.

This decision has historical precedent; stopping citizens in the course of an investigation is a practice that can be traced back to 13th-century England.

Another important aspect of arrest protocol that protects the rights of the accused is this: if someone is arrested without a warrant, he or she must receive a probable-cause hearing within 48 hours. Otherwise a suspect could be detained for an unlimited amount of

time. Even if the person is eventually found to be innocent and released, a long period of being held by the
police could have a serious impact on the person's life,
affecting his or her job, business, or family.

The authors of the Fourth Amendment sought to
protect individual freedom—but further definition of
the right to privacy is necessary for unique situations.
For example, these rights may change during an emergency. An emergency situation can involve the pursuit
of a fleeing criminal. The criminal may carry with him
"vanishing evidence"—evidence that is likely to disap-
pear before a warrant can be obtained. An example of
this might be a person suspected of driving while intox-
icated; if the suspect is not apprehended for a day or
two, there would be no way to know whether he or she
had been driving drunk. Emergency situations may also
involve children who are in trouble or property endan-
gered by fire. The government bears the burden of
proof to demonstrate that an emergency existed at the
time of the arrest.

The courts have determined as well that a person's
privacy is not protected in regard to public objects—for
instance, the sound of a person's voice, the paint on the
outside of a car, and account records held by a bank are
considered public objects.

Privacy issues change, however, when an individual
is traveling in a car. Automobiles, obviously, are
mobile; police know that if they don't look in the trunk
of a car at the time of a stop, there is a good chance
that whatever was in the trunk will be gone by the time
they secure a warrant. Nevertheless, the courts have
provided distinct stipulations about where in a car the
police can look without a warrant. For instance, they
cannot tear out the seats or look inside door panels;
they can only search a person's "wingspan"—the dis-
tance he or she could reach to stash something under
the seat while driving. However, a 1999 Supreme
Court decision expanded police authority, allowing

With probable cause, police are permitted to stop and search a person's vehicle. If the search turns up evidence that a crime is being committed, the police can arrest the driver and/or passengers, and impound the vehicle, which allows them to search it thoroughly.

officers to search containers in the car (such as packages, purses, or briefcases) if they believe they will find illegal substances, such as drugs.

If during a search the police find enough evidence to arrest the driver or passengers, they can impound the vehicle. In that case the car goes with the police, and they can take the time to search it thoroughly.

Undercover operations are another element of police work that can potentially infringe on the rights of the accused. As a practical matter, undercover police work often actually creates opportunities for people to commit crimes. Law enforcement officials may use inducement in their efforts to control drug trafficking, or they may run sting operations to catch burglars and corrupt public officials. In the case of burglaries, for example, criminals are often identified when they sell their stolen goods to police-operated fencing fronts. In 1980, an operation called Abscam targeted corrupt congressmen when an FBI agent posed as an Arab sheikh and offered bribes in exchange for political favors.

Defense lawyers have claimed that these sorts of law enforcement techniques are entrapment. In 1972 the New Mexico Court of Appeals shaped this definition of when the entrapment defense is a valid one:

> When the state's participation in the criminal enterprise reaches the point where it can be said that except for the conduct of the state a crime would probably not have been committed or because the conduct is such that it is likely to induce those to commit a crime who would normally avoid crime, or, if the conduct is such that if allowed to continue it would shake the public's confidence in the fair and honorable administration of justice, this then becomes entrapment as a matter of law.

In other words, law enforcement officials cannot encourage an otherwise innocent person to commit a crime and then arrest the person if he or she yields to temptation. The strain between preserving a person's rights and protecting society's security has many shades of gray, and when cases such as those involving surveillance and entrapment come before the courts, the difference between the criminal and the police is sometimes hard to determine. The case *Jacobson v. United States*, demonstrates how the line between good police work and overzealous efforts can get blurred.

Sixty-one-year-old Keith Jacobson, a round-faced, gray-haired man who supported his elderly father, had originally ordered two magazines and a brochure from a California adult bookstore. The magazines he ordered turned out to contain pornographic photographs of young boys. The contents of the magazines surprised Jacobson, who later testified that he had expected to receive photographs of adults. Since the boys depicted in the magazines were not engaged in sexual activity, however, Jacobson's receipt of the magazines was legal under both federal and Nebraska law.

The Supreme Court ruled that Keith Jacobson, a Nebraska farmer, had been entrapped into committing a crime by a government sting operation.

Three months later, though, the law with respect to child pornography changed. In 1984 Congress passed the Child Protection Act, which made it illegal to receive sexually explicit pictures of children through the mail. Jacobson was then the target of 26 months of mailings from government sting operators, who masqueraded as organizations dedicated to sexual freedom. Finally, after considerable government planning, Jacobson yielded to the temptations of a postal sting called Project Looking Glass and ordered a pornographic magazine that contained pictures of children. He was immediately arrested.

Jacobson's arrest drove him into seclusion for months and cost him his job. He wound up serving a two-year probation and completing some 250 hours of community service. Years later, however, in 1992, a ruling came down from the Supreme Court that reversed his conviction.

Justice Byron R. White wrote the decision for the majority court that overturned Jacobson's initial conviction. He said, "When the government's quest for convictions leads to the apprehension of an otherwise law-abiding citizen who, if left to his own devices, likely would never run afoul of the law, the courts should intervene."

Jacobson said, "I feel happy, grateful and humble. It's a victory for all Americans. It means you have a right to be let alone if you're minding your own business and not involved in some kind of criminal enterprise."

Justice Sandra Day O'Connor, however, protested the *Jacobson* decision and produced a dissenting opinion. Her concern was that the Court had introduced "a new requirement" that she believed could hamper later drug, bribery, and pornography stings. Government

agents often mimic criminal behavior to induce criminals to show their true colors. O'Connor felt that the
Jacobson decision might reduce the effectiveness of
future government sting operations.

Another less obvious law enforcement operation is
considered under the Fourth Amendment search-and-
seizure rights—the recording of a suspect's voice
through a wiretap, which is considered to be a search
under the Fourth Amendment. In order to get a valid
warrant authorizing a wiretap, the police must do
the following:

1. Police must have a showing of probable cause to believe
that a specific crime has been or is being committed;

2. The defendant whose conversations are being overheard must be named;

3. The warrant must describe the nature of the conversa-
tion that can be overheard;

4. The wiretap must be limited to a short period of time;

*Jacobson v. United States
was decided by the Supreme
Court on a 5-to-4 vote.
Justice Byron R. White
(left) wrote the majority
opinion, in which he noted
that a sting operation that
makes an otherwise law-
abiding citizen break the law
is a violation of that person's
rights. In a dissenting
opinion, Justice Sandra Day
O'Connor argued that the
ruling would hamper government operations against
drugs, child pornography,
and other illegal activities.*

5. Police have to make provisions to terminate the wiretap when the desired information has been obtained;

6. A return must be made to the court showing what conversations have been intercepted.

Most people are quite surprised at the ease with which a wiretapping can be sanctioned.

Finally, court cases in the last two decades have questioned what circumstances allow police to use deadly force to apprehend a fleeing felon. In the case *Tennessee v. Garner* (1985), the Supreme Court declared that using deadly force to apprehend a suspect constitutes a seizure—and therefore the accused is protected under the Fourth Amendment. But in their dissenting opinion Justices Sandra Day O'Connor, joined by Chief Justice Warren Burger and Justice William Rehnquist, wrote:

> Admittedly, the events giving rise to this case are in retrospect deeply regrettable. No one can view the death of an unarmed and apparently nonviolent 15-year-old without sorrow, much less disapproval. Nonetheless, the reasonableness of Officer Hymon's conduct for purposes of the Fourth Amendment cannot be evaluated by what later appears to have been a preferable course of police action. The officer pursued a suspect in the darkened backyard of a house that from all indications had been burglarized. The police officer was not certain whether the suspect was alone or unarmed; nor did he know what had transpired inside the house. He ordered the suspect to halt, and when the suspect refused to obey and attempted to flee into the night, the officer fired his weapon to prevent escape. The reasonableness of this action for purposes of the Fourth Amendment is not determined by the unfortunate nature of this particular case; instead, the question is whether it is constitutionally impermissible for police officers, as a last resort, to shoot a burglary suspect fleeing the scene of the crime.

All these narrow definitions of what is legal and what isn't may sound ridiculous; it may seem that common sense should be enough to guide the courts and law enforcement officials. However, when the courts detail what actions are illegal for law enforcement officials, they are then outlining the rights of the individual. Without this safeguarding of rights, the enormous power and resources of the government would dwarf those of the accused individual. To ensure a degree of fairness, the rights of the accused must be protected. The Fifth Amendment, discussed in the next chapter, is yet another element of the Bill of Rights that works in the accused person's favor.

The Fifth Amendment: Individual Rights

No person shall be held to answer for a capital or otherwise infamous crime, unless on a presentment or indictment of a Grand Jury, except in cases arising in the land or naval forces, or in the Militia, when in actual service in time of War or public danger; nor shall any person be subject for the same offence to be twice put in jeopardy of life or limb; nor shall be compelled in any criminal case to be a witness against himself, nor be deprived of life, liberty, or property, without due process of law; nor shall private property be taken for public use, without just compensation.

One night in the early spring of 1963 a woman (known in court reports as Lois Ann Jameson) was on her way home from work at the Paramount Theater in downtown Phoenix, Arizona, when her life changed forever. She stepped off the bus a few minutes after midnight, heading toward

Ernesto Miranda was the central figure in a landmark case that defined police arrest procedure.

home, when a car suddenly pulled out of a driveway and blocked her path. The driver dragged her into his car, tied her hands and ankles, and warned her not to move. In an outlying desert area she was forced to undress, and then she was raped and robbed of four dollars. Later she was allowed to get dressed and return to the neighborhood where she had been abducted.

On March 4, 1963, Detective Carroll Cooley of the Phoenix Metro Police Department began his investigation of this crime. Evidence soon led law enforcement officials to the home of Twila Hoffman, who lived in the nearby suburb of Mesa, Arizona. Hoffman lived with a man named Ernest Miranda, who roughly fit the description of Jameson's assailant. Checking Miranda's work record, police found that he had been absent from his job at United Produce on the night of the crime. Further investigation uncovered the fact that Miranda had a rather lengthy criminal record.

Cooley and another policeman, Wilfred Young, went to Twila Hoffman's residence, and there they asked Miranda to accompany them downtown to the police station to discuss a case they were investigating. At police headquarters Miranda participated in a lineup and was identified by Lois Ann Jameson. Detectives informed Miranda he had been identified and began questioning him in greater detail.

The detectives would later tell the courts that "neither threats nor promises had been made" toward Miranda, who eventually admitted he had raped Jameson and then confessed to a second robbery. The entire interrogation took a little more than two hours, and at the end of this time Miranda signed a written confession. There was no evidence of police brutality or anything else out of the ordinary.

Ernest Miranda was charged with kidnapping and rape, put on trial, and sentenced to concurrent prison terms (sentences that are served simultaneously, rather than one after the other) of 20 to 30 years for each

In Miranda v. Arizona (1966), the Supreme Court's chief justice, Earl Warren, called the Fifth Amendment right against self-incrimination a mainstay of the legal system.

charge, to be served at the Arizona State Prison. Less than three years later, however, the *Miranda* case was at the center of a landmark Supreme Court decision that changed the standard of police arrest procedure forever.

Essentially, Miranda's conviction was overturned because the police had not advised him about his Fifth Amendment rights—that is, the right to remain silent to avoid self-incrimination, and the right to receive advice from an attorney before answering police questions—at the beginning of his interrogation. In effect, failing to provide suspects with this information infringes on their rights. Today, whenever police officers arrest a suspect, they must clearly inform the suspect of the rights guaranteed by the Fifth

Amendment. This information has become known as the Miranda warnings.

In *Miranda v. Arizona*, the Supreme Court recognized the effects an interrogation by police can have on a suspect. In his majority opinion Chief Justice Earl Warren wrote, "The atmosphere and environment of incommunicado interrogation as it exists today is inherently intimidating and works to undermine the privilege against self-incrimination." Warren went on to call the right against self-incrimination a mainstay of the legal system, pointing out that it guarantees the individual the "right to remain silent unless he chooses to speak in the unfettered exercise of his own free will."

Among the many provisions in the Fifth Amendment is the right of protection against self-incrimination. The amendment reads, in part, "No person . . . shall be compelled in any criminal case to be a witness against himself." This concept is most important when it comes to interrogation. Under the protection of the Fifth Amendment, no person can be abused or tortured in order to give a confession. To secure the validity of a confession, suspects must be notified of their right against self-incrimination and their right to legal counsel.

Because of this, certain obstacles must be removed before any self-incriminating statements can be introduced as evidence. For example, the prosecutor must demonstrate that the confession was not forced from the person in any way. Also, incriminating statements may not be admitted if the accused did not waive the right to counsel, or if the suspect made the statement without first being advised of his or her Fifth Amendment rights (as the *Miranda* case established). Finally, the prosecutor must show that the defendant understood his or her rights and knowingly waived them before making self-incriminating statements.

After the Supreme Court's *Miranda* ruling, police officials began to complain that the Court had placed

DEFENDANT

LOCATION

SPECIFIC WARNING REGARDING INTERROGATIONS

1. YOU HAVE THE RIGHT TO REMAIN SILENT.

2. ANYTHING YOU SAY CAN AND WILL BE USED AGAINST YOU IN A COURT OF LAW.

3. YOU HAVE THE RIGHT TO TALK TO A LAWYER AND HAVE HIM PRESENT WITH YOU WHILE YOU ARE BEING QUESTIONED.

4. IF YOU CANNOT AFFORD TO HIRE A LAWYER ONE WILL BE APPOINTED TO REPRESENT YOU BEFORE ANY QUESTIONING, IF YOU WISH ONE.

SIGNATURE OF DEFENDANT

DATE

WITNESS

TIME

☐ REFUSED SIGNATURE   SAN FRANCISCO POLICE DEPARTMENT   PR.9.1.4

the rights of criminal suspects over those of society. The reason behind the Supreme Court's decision, however, was that law enforcement would be made more reliable if criminal prosecutions were founded on independently obtained evidence, rather than on confessions secured under coercive interrogation and without benefit of legal counsel.

In 1968 an exception to the *Miranda* ruling was allowed. The Omnibus Crime Control and Safe Streets Act provided that in federal cases a voluntary confession could be used as evidence even if the accused person was not informed of his or her rights. As a result, confessions have been allowed in evidence under certain circumstances. This has extended to both federal and state courts.

In the 1980s another ruling shifted the legal system to further restrict individual rights. In the case *New York v. Quarles* (1984), the question was raised as to

A card adopted by the San Francisco Police Department shortly after the Miranda decision shows the Fifth Amendment warnings that the court required police officers to give all criminal suspects. Typically, the four warnings shown on this card are followed by the explanation that the suspect can decide at any time to exercise these rights and not answer questions or make statements. After the warnings are read, the police can ask if the accused understands his Fifth Amendment rights and wishes to waive those rights and answer questions.

whether a police officer could ask a suspect for his or her gun before issuing the Miranda warnings. The Court affirmed that this procedure for securing the gun was all right, because police were applying a concern for safety in a public place over the rights of an accused individual. Many agreed that this was a necessary decision; by establishing that disarming a suspect was not a violation of his or her Fifth Amendment rights, this ruling provided protection for police officers and other citizens who might be in the area where the arrest was taking place.

Some critics of *Miranda* imply that criminals are going free simply because the police neglected to read them their rights. However, this is incorrect. Any statements made by the accused that are in violation of his or her Fifth Amendment rights will be inadmissible as evidence in a trial, but this does not necessarily mean that the charges will be dropped. If the prosecutor has other evidence that can be used against the suspect, the case will certainly be pursued. However, if the evidence is dependent on a tainted interrogation that was obtained in violation of the suspect's Fifth Amendment rights, then any verdict can be overturned, as the Gary Gauger case in chapter 1 demonstrated.

An important early precedent was set in 1963. Police in California were investigating a series of purse-snatch robberies. One of the victims died as a result of the injuries inflicted by her assailant, making the assailant guilty of murder as well as robbery. He then made the mistake of endorsing a check taken in one of his robberies, and bank authorities alerted police of his activity. On the evening of January 31, 1963, police officers went to Roy Allen Stewart's home and arrested him. Upon arrival one of the officers asked Stewart if they could search the house, and Stewart replied, "Go ahead." The search turned up various items taken from the five robbery victims.

At the time of Stewart's arrest police also arrested

Stewart's wife and three other persons who were visit-
ing. The four were taken to jail, along with Stewart,
and questioned. Then Stewart was taken to the University Station of the Los Angeles Police Department,
where he was placed in a cell. During the next five days
police interrogated Stewart on nine different occasions.
On one occasion Stewart was confronted by an accusing witness; during the other sessions he was isolated
with his interrogators.

Sometime during the ninth interrogation, Stewart
broke down and admitted that he had robbed the
deceased woman but claimed he had not meant to hurt
her. Police then brought Stewart before a magistrate for
the first time. The other four people arrested with
Stewart were released for lack of involvement.

Nothing in the record indicated Stewart had been
advised of his right to remain silent or his right to
counsel. In follow-up the interrogating officers were
asked to recount their conversations, and no one men-
tioned that Stewart had been advised of his Fifth
Amendment rights.

In court the jury found Stewart guilty of robbery
and first-degree murder, and he was sentenced to death.
On appeal, though, the Supreme Court of California
reversed the decision on the basis that Stewart should
have been advised of his right to remain silent and his
right to counsel. The Court said it could not presume,
in the face of a silent record, that the police had per-
formed the required Fifth Amendment advisements,
"nor can a knowing and intelligent waiver of these
rights be assumed on a silent record. Furthermore,
Stewart's steadfast denial of the alleged offenses
through eight of the nine interrogations over a period
of five days is subject to no other construction than
that he was compelled by persistent interrogation to
forgo his Fifth Amendment privilege." Stewart was
allowed to go free.

Another of the protections provided by the Fifth

Prospective grand jurors line up outside the Queens (New York) County Courthouse. New York is one of the few states in which nearly every criminal case is reviewed by a 23-member grand jury. About 25,000 people serve on New York grand juries each year.

Amendment is the assurance that anyone accused of a "capital or otherwise infamous crime" will not be held for trial unless indicted by a grand jury. A grand jury is made up of a number of private citizens selected to review and investigate felony cases. Traditionally, a grand jury consists of 23 persons and requires a majority vote to indict.

In the case *United States v. Dionisio* (1973) the Supreme Court proclaimed that the purpose of the grand jury is to stand between government agents and the suspect as an unbiased evaluator of evidence. In theory the grand jury should protect suspects from indictments based on weak or unsubstantiated evidence presented by the prosecutor. Grand juries have the power to conduct their own investigation into important cases, rather than simply depending on the prosecutor to provide evidence.

In grand jury proceedings, however, the target of the investigation is not afforded the normal due process rights that a criminal suspect receives at the police station or in the courtroom. This is because the grand jury merely decides if there is enough evidence to allow a case to go to trial; it does not determine a defendant's guilt or innocence.

The grand jury system and due process rights are two of the great advantages given to private citizens to protect them from the dangers of an overzealous prosecutor. They help tip the scales in favor of individual rights over public safety.

The Fifth Amendment also contains a clause saying that no person shall be "subject for the same offence to be twice put in jeopardy of life or limb." This is our constitutional prohibition against what has been called "double jeopardy." Basically it means that if the defendant is found not guilty at trial, he or she cannot be tried again for the same offense, even if overwhelming evidence comes in later that proves his or her guilt.

But, as with every other law, there are exceptions here, too. For example, when the first case ends, with the defendant's consent, in a mistrial, he or she can be tried again for the same offense in the same courtroom. A defendant can also be tried twice for the same offense if the first case was dismissed for some reason, either at trial or during trial but before acquittal. If the trial has already begun, the dismissal must be based on a reason other than the defendant's guilt or innocence. And finally, if a defendant is convicted and then appeals his or her case to a higher court, and the higher court reverses the conviction based on an error made in the first trial and orders a new trial, the defendant has waived his or her

The Fifth Amendment protects the accused from "double jeopardy"—being tried twice for the same crime. Once a person has been acquitted of a crime, he or she can never be tried for that offense again.

claim to double jeopardy simply by initiating the appeals process. In the case of appeals one additional consideration applies: the new trial must be for the same offense, and not for a greater offense or a greater degree of offense. For example, a person who is being retried on charges that he or she committed a class B felony (such as robbery) cannot also be tried at the same time for a class A felony (such as murder), because each class of felony carries a different level of punishment.

The Fifth Amendment is loaded with promises, rules, and guarantees that are important to the rights of the accused. Despite these rights, the defendant may not fully realize that in preparation for an investigation and subsequent trial the balance of power now goes against him or her. While the prosecution can freely grant immunity and compel witnesses to testify, the defense has no such power. It can only protect the defendant against third-degree tactics, hope for reliable evidence, and depend on the wisdom of the judge and jury to sort things out. However, the Sixth Amendment, which will be discussed next, does give the defendant one important protection: the right to legal counsel.

THE SIXTH AMENDMENT: RIGHTS IN CRIMINAL PROSECUTIONS

In all criminal prosecutions, the accused shall enjoy the right to a speedy and public trial, by an impartial jury of the State and district wherein the crime shall have been committed, which district shall have been previously ascertained by law, and to be informed of the nature and cause of the accusation; to be confronted with the witnesses against him; to have compulsory process for obtaining witnesses in his favor, and to have the Assistance of Counsel for his defence.

It would be nearly impossible for a citizen who has no knowledge of the law to defend him- or herself in court. The Sixth Amendment says that the government must provide legal counsel to all persons accused of crime if they are unable to afford an attorney.

Just before dawn on June 3, 1961, in Panama City, Florida, a police officer was making his rounds when he noticed that the front door of the Bay Harbor Poolroom was slightly open. Upon investigation he discovered the rear window of the building had been shattered and a cigarette machine and a jukebox had apparently been robbed.

A local bystander informed the policeman that he

had seen a man named Clarence Gideon in the pool-room earlier. On the basis of this information Gideon was arrested and charged with breaking and entering with intent to commit a misdemeanor, a felony under Florida law.

Gideon had been convicted and served time for a variety of previous offenses, including burglary, possession of government property, and attempted burglary. He had escaped from prison, was captured, and then served a full term, only to repeat another burglary in a different state.

After the Florida poolroom incident, the defendant requested that the court provide counsel for him because, Gideon argued, he was destitute and could not afford to pay a lawyer. Judge Robert L. McCrary Jr. denied his application. Under Florida law and the federal constitutional precedent at the time, the court was required to appoint counsel only to represent a defendant charged with a capital offense (a crime that holds the potential for the death penalty).

Unable to muster the forces needed for legal defense, Gideon was sentenced to the maximum penalty of five years' imprisonment. Still without counsel, Gideon proceeded to teach himself the law and made appeals on his own behalf. Gideon's appeal, handwritten in pencil on notebook paper, eventually caught the attention of the Supreme Court.

This time Gideon did have counsel when his petition was heard during the Supreme Court's 1962–63 term. A successful Washington lawyer, Abe Fortas, was appointed to the case. In its decision the Supreme Court stated, "[R]eason and reflection require us to recognize that in our adversary system, the accused cannot be assured a fair trial unless counsel is provided for him." As a result, Gideon was acquitted when he was finally retried with counsel.

Over the years various rulings have come down pertaining to this principle of counsel. Today, failure to

The case of Clarence Gideon, a mechanic and jack-of-all-trades accused of robbery in Florida, forever changed the American legal system.

provide a defendant with legal counsel during a trial means an automatic reversal of any conviction, even without showing any specific unfairness in the proceeding. At nontrial proceedings, though, defendants must show they were actually harmed as a result of their denial to counsel.

The primary responsibility of the defense attorney is to represent his or her client, who has the constitutional right to legal counsel. If defenders are asked the

A copy of Gideon's hand-written appeal to the Supreme Court. The Court ruled in Gideon v. Wainwright *that "the accused cannot be assured a fair trial unless counsel is provided for him." In a retrial, with the assistance of a defense attorney, Gideon was acquitted of the charges.*

DIVISION OF CORRECTIONS
CORRESPONDENCE REGULATIONS

MAIL WILL NOT BE DELIVERED WHICH DOES NOT CONFORM WITH THESE RULES

No. 1 -- Only 2 letters each week, not to exceed 2 sheets letter-size 8 1/2 x 11" and written *on one side only*, and if ruled paper, do not write between lines. *Your complete name* must be signed at the close of your letter. *Clippings, stamps, letters* from other people, *stationery* or *cash* must not be enclosed in your letters.

No. 2 -- All *letters* must be addressed in the *complete prison name* of the inmate. *Cell number*, where applicable, and *prison number* must be placed in lower left corner of envelope, with your complete name and address in the upper left corner.

No. 3 -- Do not send any *packages* without a *Package Permit*. Unauthorized *packages* will be destroyed.

No. 4 -- *Letters* must be written in English only.

No. 5 -- *Books, magazines, pamphlets,* and *newspapers* of reputable character will be delivered only *if* mailed direct from the publisher.

No. 6 -- *Money* must be sent in the form of *Postal Money Orders* only, in the inmate's complete prison name and prison number.

INSTITUTION _____   CELL NUMBER _____

NAME _____   NUMBER _____

In The Supreme Court of The United States
Washington D.C.
Clarence Earl Gideon
      Petitioner
      vs.   Petition for a writ
H.G. Cochran, Jr, as   of Certiorari Directed
Director, Divisions   to The Supreme Court
of corrections State   State of Florida.
of Florida   No. 890 Misc.

OCT. TERM 1961
U.S. Supreme Court

To. The Honorable Earl Warren, Chief
      Justice of the United States
      Comes now The petitioner, Clarence
Earl Gideon, a citizen of The United States
of America, in proper person, and appearing
as his own counsel. Who petitions This
Honorable Court for a Writ of Certiorari
directed to The Supreme Court of The State
of Florida. To review the order and Judge-
ment of the court below denying The
petitioner a writ of Habeus Corpus.
      Petitioner submits That The Supreme
Court of the United States has The authority
and jurisdiction to review the final Judge-
ment of The Supreme Court of The State
of Florida the highest court of The State
Under sec. 344(B) Title 28 U.S.C.A. and
Because The "Due process clause" of the

one credo they live by, this is the ritualized speech they most often give: "The rights of the accused were designed to protect the innocent, and if the guilty are freed as a result of some technical issue, then that is the price that must be paid in order to ensure that the scales of justice remain balanced."

Today we assume that defendants facing criminal charges need a lawyer to assist them. The law and its procedures are confusing, and the tasks required to facilitate fairness require a level of expertise most citizens do not have. In order to understand the nature and consequences of the proceedings, to navigate the intricacies of courtroom operations, the accused person needs help from someone who knows the system. According to the American Bar Association, the defense attorney performs a multitude of functions while representing a client throughout the entire criminal proceeding. Some of these functions include

- representing the accused immediately after arrest, providing advice during interrogation, and ensuring that constitutional safeguards are in place during pretrial procedures
- reviewing police reports and conducting further investigation
- interviewing the police and witnesses, and seeking additional evidence and details from the accused
- discussing the unfolding events with the prosecutor in the hope of gaining insight into the strength of the case against their client
- representing the accused at all bail hearings and during plea negotiations
- preparing, filing, and arguing pretrial motions
- preparing the case for trial and representing the accused at trial
- participating in jury selection
- providing advice and assistance at sentencing
- determining an appropriate basis for appeal, and processing the appeal
- presenting written or oral arguments for appeal

The average person simply does not know enough about the rules and laws involved in a case to create an adequate defense. That is why, to protect the rights of the accused, all defendants need to be guaranteed legal counsel, whether or not they can afford to pay a lawyer.

Unfortunately, however, there are problems with

government-appointed lawyers. Most states pay so poorly for public defenders that many in the field of justice feel that a client with a court-appointed lawyer stands to get much less in terms of defense. Virginia's public defender allotment fee provides an example of this problem.

"What Virginia pays court-appointed defense lawyers is abysmally, disgracefully low," says Lynchburg prosecutor Bill Perry, a former president of the Commonwealth Attorneys Association, the prosecutors' trade group. Perry claims that public defenders lose money unless a case is resolved quickly—and the best way to bring a case to a close is with a guilty plea. As a result, public defenders may counsel their clients to submit a plea that is not in fact in the defendant's best interests. Dennis Dohnal, chairman of a committee appointed by the state supreme court to study the problem, says, "I'd like to think that lawyers aren't cutting corners. But the reality is shortcuts get taken."

While there are exceptions, usually the only attorneys who will take on public-generated work are young lawyers seeking a training ground for future litigation, or unscrupulous attorneys who are looking for profits by using the quick-turnover formula to generate a volume of clients. Does this sort of defense actually protect the Sixth Amendment rights of the accused?

The fact remains, however, that the right to counsel is guaranteed to anyone who is accused of a crime. Despite this fact, many people have confused this right with other guarantees that the amendment does not in fact make. One popular misconception is that an arrested person is entitled to one phone call. Based on what we see on television shows and in movies, most of us believe that after an arrest police have to let the accused person make one phone call to anyone he or she chooses. This is simply not true. The only person the accused has the right to contact is an attorney— and the police must allow more than one phone call to

For nearly 800 years, since the signing of the Magna Carta by King John of England in 1215, the right of trial by jury has been an essential part of judicial systems. The Constitution of the United States guarantees that "the trial of all Crimes . . . shall be by Jury."

an attorney if necessary. As a matter of common decency, public goodwill, and in order to maintain the peace within most jails, corrections officers do usually allow the accused to contact most anyone by phone, and—within visitation guidelines—will allow nonattorney visitors on an unlimited basis. But this is not a right specified in the Sixth Amendment or anywhere else in the Constitution.

Not only does the Sixth Amendment guarantee the accused's right to legal counsel, it also holds that "in all criminal prosecutions, the accused shall enjoy the right to a speedy and public trial, by an impartial jury." The selection of a jury is the primary phase of any criminal trial. For the accused, now the defendant, it is probably the most important procedure.

The right to a trial by jury is a distinctive feature in the system of jurisprudence, dating back more than seven centuries. The English Magna Carta of 1215 contained the stipulation that no freeholder could be deprived of life or property except by judgment of his peers. Article 3 of the Constitution incorporates this principle with the following statement: "The trial of all Crimes, except in Cases of Impeachment, shall be by Jury."

The accused also have the right to dispense with a jury and can request to be tried by a judge alone. These trials are called bench trials. In some states defendants must file a request for a jury trial either when they enter a plea or at some time before the beginning of a court term in which a jury would be impaneled. Failure to file constitutes a waiver of the right. In all criminal matters in which jail is a potential penalty, though, the accused have an absolute right to a jury trial.

The primary purpose of a jury is to serve as a check against arbitrary or vindictive law enforcement. Few other nations besides the United States allow ordinary citizens the responsibility to decide a criminal defendant's ultimate fate. Of course, judges still have power; precedent (or previous law) helps them define the rules of law and the sentencing guidelines, providing them with discretionary authority.

Both the defense and the prosecution are given a list of the potential jurors. Around 120 names will be on the call-up list, so an initial examination of them is difficult. A much smaller percentage will be represented in court on the day of the trial, and from this pool 14 names (12 jurors and 2 alternates) will be drawn at random from the attendees. This first batch

will undergo a voir dire examination by the judge and the attorneys for both sides.

Voir dire, an Old French term meaning "to speak truly," is the process of questioning the jurors by both opposing attorneys. The process is meant to ferret out those jurors who will act fairly and remain unbiased. The prosecution and the defense are each allowed a specific number of peremptory challenges; in other words, they are allowed to remove prospective jurors from their duty with no explanation given. Jurors can also be removed for "cause"—this occurs when some fact is disclosed that would make the prospective juror unfit to serve. A relationship between one of the jurors and a witness may be cause for dismissal. People who have strong feelings, either positive or negative, about alcohol, religion, guns, or certain ethnic groups might also be dismissed, depending on the details of the case,

The members of a jury are drawn from a larger pool, and attorneys for both the prosecution and the defense are allowed to question the potential jurors. Some potential jurors can be eliminated for "cause"; others may be removed from consideration by peremptory challenges, which require no explanation. Here, the members of a jury are sworn in before a trial.

if the attorneys feel the potential juror's beliefs will interfere with a fair judgment. In cases involving a capital offense, such as murder, jurors are often subjected to complex questions about their attitudes toward the death penalty. A juror who could never vote to put a defendant to death is likely to be excused for cause, as is one who would always vote for death for any defendant convicted of murder.

The Sixth Amendment's guarantee of "the right to a speedy and public trial" really serves two purposes—one that protects the individual's interests and one that protects society's. Although some defendants may feel their trial occurs altogether too quickly, a speedy trial relieves a defendant of the long-term consequences involved with being accused. If the accused is subject to incarceration while awaiting trial, any length of time in jail seems oppressive—not to mention the drain of personal finances it may cause, as well as the loss of a job or business, family problems, and feelings of personal anxiety. The second purpose promotes society's interest in the prompt disposition of charges. Law-abiding citizens are often concerned that justice be administered in a proper and timely manner, especially when a crime occurs in their own neighborhood; they may feel threatened by the unresolved details surrounding the crime, or they may fear additional harm to the community should the perpetrator be on the loose. A speedy trial is the answer to these fears.

The right to a speedy trial, however, begins only after a person has been formally accused of a crime—after he or she has been indicted and taken into custody. A delay in filing charges against a suspect does not violate his or her right to a speedy trial. Once the accused person is arrested, however, he or she is entitled to a speedy trial, even if he or she is subsequently released and not indicted for a substantial period of time.

The actual amount of time that would be "speedy" is the judge's call. The conduct of both the prosecution and the defense must be weighed by a judge, who also considers additional factors, such as the length of delay, the reason for the delay, whether the defendant has asked for or waived the right to a speedy trial, and whether or not the delay will hurt the defendant's case in some way. For example, if the delay created a lengthy period of jail time for the defendant that resulted in the loss of evidence, the death of a witness, inaccurate witness testimony, or a measurably increased anxiety level for the accused, then the judge would be more likely to determine that the defendant did not receive a trial quickly enough.

Length of delay alone does not establish a violation, because unless the delay has been sufficiently long enough to be prejudicial, there is no need to examine the other relevant factors. Some states, however, have specific time limits within which an accused person must be brought to trial. In Florida, for example, a defendant who is not incarcerated must go to trial within 120 days, while an accused person who is in jail has an even shorter trial date time limit—90 days.

The reason for the delay is also legally significant. If the prosecutor deliberately attempts to delay the trial to his advantage (for example, using the extra time to find additional facts that would help prove his case), the defendant's claim that his right to a speedy trial has been violated will probably be seriously considered. However, if the delay is sustained through efforts by the accused, then the accused will be deemed to have waived his right to a speedy trial.

The Sixth Amendment also provides that in all criminal prosecutions the accused shall have the right to a public trial. The authors of the amendment had good reason to safeguard this right; their experiences as British colonists before the American Revolution had taught them to distrust any secret government activity. The purpose of a public trial is to guard against any attempts to use the courts as instruments of prosecu-

News reporters swarm around a suspect leaving a courthouse. While citizens are guaranteed the right to a public trial, in some cases the judge may feel it necessary to close the proceedings to the media.

tion, allowing citizens to know any actions that have been taken against one of them. In certain instances, however, trials take place as closed proceedings. Judges have the ability to exclude members of the public from the trial if they feel they have reason to do so (for example, if the trial has to do with a rape, or if it involves youthful offenders). In 1990, for instance, a New York trial case of an investment banker who had been gang-raped was closed to spectators during the victim's testimony, and her name was never revealed by the media.

An area of current concern is whether to bar news reporters from a trial. The courts have said that even if the government, the defendant, and the judge have all agreed to a closed hearing, members of the media could invoke the First, Fifth, and Sixth Amendments as reasons they should be allowed to attend the proceedings. Because of this, rules have been determined to establish when members of the media can and cannot attend a trial.

The right to confront witnesses is also protected by the Sixth Amendment. This confrontation provision serves three purposes: First, the oath helps ensure the reliability of the witnesses' testimonies. Second, confrontation exposes the witnesses to further examination by means of the defense's cross-examination. And finally, it allows the judge and jury a chance to weigh the demeanor of the witnesses and helps them discern credibility.

Since the right to confront witnesses is deemed a fundamental right in federal prosecutions, it is applicable to state law as well under the Fourteenth Amendment's due process clause. This clause includes the right of the accused to be physically present during the course of a trial. However, the accused can also waive this right by voluntarily absenting himself or herself from the proceedings.

The right to confront witnesses is essentially the right to cross-examine witnesses, but here the accused generally relies on the defense lawyer. Being able to cross-examine witnesses is an important, and difficult, skill to master and one of the more significant methods used by the trial attorney. When witnesses claim to tell the truth as they know it, that truth may be tainted because of their viewpoint. Answers to questions may be skewed for many reasons—witnesses may be trying to shield themselves or hide their own actions, they may have a desire to punish the accused, or they may simply be confused or misinformed. Witnesses may not want to accept the basic principle of our legal system, that the accused is "innocent until proven guilty." It is up to the defense attorney to reveal the truth through careful questioning. He or she must separate opinions from facts, and has the right to impeach the witness's own words or to present an alternate theory to the crime.

Since the mere omission of testimony could be damaging, the Sixth Amendment contains another provision that protects the accused's rights. Although this provision is not spelled out, the amendment nevertheless makes the right to confront witnesses compulsory rather than optional. Just as the prosecutor has the power to subpoena witnesses on the state's behalf, the defendant has the right to compel someone to come to court to give testimony. Even in the case where a witness has been deported, if that person's testimony is an important factor in the defendant's defense, then the defense gets another trial at which the witness must appear.

The accused faces other risks in the trial process as well. What if the trial judge makes threatening remarks that drive the only defense witness off the stand? Or what if the government decides to deport a witness? The Supreme Court said in *Webb v. Texas* (1972) that the tactic of the threatening judge in effect prevents the accused from presenting his or her witnesses and their version of the facts, and therefore it cannot be allowed.

Furthermore, the Supreme Court has ruled that exclusion of crucial defense evidence by the trial judge impairs the right of the accused to present a defense, even when the evidence offered is technically inadmissible under appropriate local rules. For example, in *Chambers v. Mississippi* (1973) the defendant offered evidence that the crime he was accused of had been committed by someone else, and he had an oral confession to prove it. The evidence was excluded on the grounds that it was hearsay under the rules of evidence. The Supreme Court reversed that decision, saying that if the evidence was held back, it would impair the defendant's right to present a defense.

However, not every witness can be compelled to testify, since some information is considered "privileged." Privileged communications are those protected

by law, such as things that are said between an attorney and his or her client, or a priest and the penitent. The person on the receiving end of the information cannot be compelled to divulge the content of the communication unless the person doing the confiding waives his or her legal right to secrecy. Likewise, private talks between husband and wife are also privileged, although in some states people are allowed to testify on behalf of their spouse.

Confidential conversations, however, are different from privileged ones. Confidentiality refers simply to an ethical obligation on the part of a skilled specialist to safeguard information given by a client in a professional capacity. These confidential conversations have no legal protection in the court, unless they can be

Persons accused of a crime are permitted to review the prosecutor's evidence against them before the case goes to trial.

considered privileged communications as well. For example, a marriage counselor ethically should not divulge any statements made by a client. But in the courtroom venue, the information the counselor possesses is not considered privileged, and he or she will be compelled to tell or risk a contempt of court citation (such as a fine or imprisonment) from the judge.

In every jurisdiction the prosecution has to tell the accused and his or her counsel what evidence it intends to use against him or her during the trial. This is information included in pretrial discovery. In some cases the prosecution will turn over copies of its pretrial discovery information voluntarily; in others, the accused's attorneys may have to make a motion or file a pleading to obtain it. The file should include the names of witnesses and their addresses, as well as any prior criminal activity on the part of these witnesses. Also, a list of documents or other exhibits that will be used against the accused as evidence in court will generally be in the discovery package. The accused should take this process seriously, because the prosecution is also obligated to turn over any evidence it has that might establish the defendant's innocence or at least point to other police leads in the case. For example, perhaps something that might be used to exonerate the accused has turned up, or maybe the police failed to investigate other persons who might have committed the crime. The accused has a right to examine the records, police reports, and other scientific materials. Most prosecutors will reveal this evidence to the extent required by local rules.

All in all, the Sixth Amendment, like the other amendments that have been discussed, does much to protect the rights of the accused. Still, many Americans disagree about whether so much emphasis should be placed on these rights by our legal system. Critics argue that some of the provisions of these amendments in effect allow criminals to go free, threatening the safety of the public. If there is an element of truth in this criticism, then should our legal system abandon its long tug-of-war between individual freedom and public safety? In today's dangerous world, has the time finally come to award the victory, once and for all, to the side of stability and security over private freedom?

RIGHTS VERSUS SECURITY

I n the early 1960s police received information that a man named Antonio Richard Rochin was selling narcotics. Based on this report three officers went to his home, where they forced open the door of his room. They found Rochin partially dressed, sitting on the side of the bed, next to where his wife was lying.

On a nightstand beside the bed the policemen spied two capsules. When the lawmen asked, "Whose stuff is this?" Rochin seized the capsules and put them in his mouth. A struggle ensued in which the three officers attempted to extract the capsules from his mouth. Instead, Rochin swallowed them.

The suspect was then handcuffed and taken away. However, the policemen did not take him to jail;

To create a safe society, police must be able to enforce the laws effectively. However, the need for broad police powers must be balanced with a concern for, and protection of, the rights of individuals accused of crime.

Rochin was taken to a hospital instead. Under instructions from one of the officers, a doctor forced an emetic solution (a mixture that causes vomiting) through a tube into Rochin's stomach—against his will. This technique, also called stomach pumping, worked in the desired manner, and two undigested capsules containing morphine were found in the vomited matter.

In 1963, Rochin was convicted of possessing morphine and sentenced to 60 days' imprisonment. The chief evidence against him was the existence of the two capsules.

However, the case didn't end there, because Rochin's lawyers appealed the decision; his case eventually reached the U.S. Supreme Court. In 1966 the Supreme Court decided that when the police forcibly pumped Rochin's stomach, they had violated due process of law. Justice Felix Frankfurter wrote the Court's official opinion on the case, in which he concluded that Rochin's protection from unreasonable search and seizure, guaranteed by the Constitution's Fourth Amendment, had been violated. Frankfurter wrote:

> This is conduct that shocks the conscience. Illegally breaking into the privacy of the petitioner, the struggle to open his mouth and remove what was there, the forcible extraction of his stomach's contents—this course of proceeding by agents of government to obtain evidence is bound to offend even hardened sensibilities. They are methods too close to the rack and the screw to permit of constitutional differentiation.

Another Justice, William O. Douglas, wrote a separate, concurring opinion on this case. Douglas noted that the stomach pumping violated Rochin's Fifth Amendment rights as well, those which protect citizens from self-incrimination. He maintained that because of this protection, "words taken from [an accused's] lips, capsules taken from his stomach, blood taken from his veins are all inadmissible provided they are taken from him without consent. [This] is an

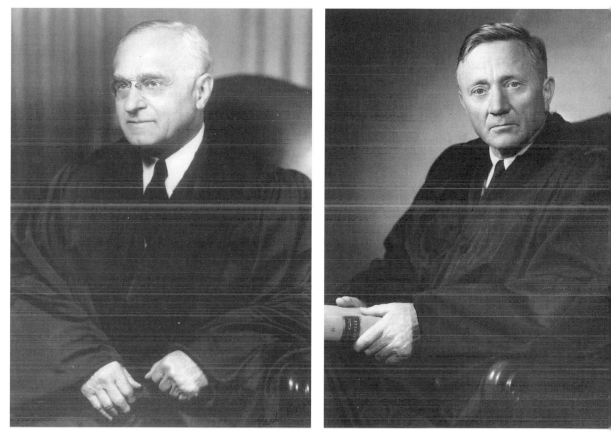

unequivocal, definite and workable rule of evidence for state and federal courts."

Was Rochin guilty of the crime of which he was convicted? Yes, he was. But in this case a guilty man went free because of an error made by the authorities when they collected evidence. Rochin's guilt was never in question. The evidence clearly showed that Rochin had broken the law by possessing an illegal substance, a crime for which millions of people are currently in prison.

Many people agree that a guilty verdict in the Rochin case would have undermined many of the rights taken for granted by citizens of the United States. Still, others feel that our nation has gone too far to protect the rights of accused criminals. The tug-of-

In Rochin vs. California (1966), the Supreme Court found that the police had gone too far in their pursuit of evidence. Justice Felix Frankfurter (left) wrote the Court's official opinion, in which he noted that law enforcement officials had violated Rochin's Fourth Amendment rights. Another justice, William O. Douglas, wrote a separate, concurring opinion in which he argued that Rochin's Fifth Amendment protection had been violated as well.

war between these two opposing points of view goes back and forth, with first one side gaining ground and then the other.

For example, Norman Kinne, assistant district attorney in Dallas, Texas, and Peter Lesser, a criminal defense attorney in Dallas, each have differing opinions. Lesser says that the Bill of Rights ensures that citizens have protection from government. The system was designed to prevent abuses, and he believes we have seen a consistent eroding of rights by the courts. Meanwhile, Kinne, on the other hand, says that we have gone too far to ensure the accused of their rights, and we are coping poorly with the conflict between public security and private rights. He says that the American people feel differently about justice than do the judicial authorities who hand down their decisions. The public, Kinne feels, demands more victims' rights, while in his opinion the courts are currently offering more rights to the accused.

Kinne and Lesser have different passions about the interpretation of law. These opposing passions help to illustrate the dichotomy between a society's need for security and that same society's long-standing desire to extend rights to the individual who has been accused of breaking the law. Inevitably those rights will enable some people who are guilty to escape punishment. Unfortunately, the protection offered to each side of the rights-versus-security issue is not perfect in either case. The stories about lives that have fallen through the cracks are all too common, as the next two cases illustrate.

♣   ♣   ♣

Late one fall night in 1990, New York state troopers saw a van zoom by them at 70 miles an hour. The police officers chased the vehicle down, and then they asked to look in the back of the van. Hunting season was under way, and they were looking for illegal deer carcasses or loaded hunting guns; what they found, however, was the body of Fernando Cuervo, who had been shot to death. The driver, Leonardo Turriago, was arrested.

The evidence against Turriago was overwhelming. Not only did police have the body, they also found the murder weapon that had been tossed into the Hudson River, and they found drugs and guns in Turriago's New York City apartment. He was convicted of Cuervo's murder and sentenced to 45 years to life in prison.

In June 1996, however, Turriago's conviction was appealed and overturned. The state appeals court ruled that the troopers' search of Turriago's van had been illegal, since they had no warrant, nor did they have "founded suspicion that criminality was afoot." In other words, until they looked in the back of the van, the troopers had no reason to think that Turriago was guilty of anything except speeding. The court ruled that the search of the van was illegal—which made the dead body "fruit of the poisonous tree" (a concept discussed in chapter 3 that says any evidence uncovered illegally is not admissible in court). Turriago was free to go.

People were outraged at this decision. Turriago was clearly a murderer—and yet he had been released on a technicality. Critics of our legal system who claim public security is more important than individual rights seized this case as an illustration of a dangerous trend within our courts. These critics claim that American law has gone way too far in protecting the rights of the accused.

Actually, the Turriago case is extreme. New York State's requirement that police have "founded suspicion" for a warrantless search is unusual; most state laws, as well as the federal courts, would have deemed the search legal simply because Turriago did initially consent to it. Unfortunately, though, his is not the only case where a defendant who was clearly guilty went free because of a technicality of law.

However, the fact remains that these laws were ini-

Verneal Jimerson (left), Dennis Williams (center), and Kenny Adams (right) were released from a Chicago prison in 1996 after spending 18 years in jail for a crime that they did not commit.

tially designed to protect innocent people, not guilty ones, to keep them from being unjustly accused by a too powerful government. We do not want innocent people railroaded into jail by unchecked law enforcement powers; we want to protect the rights of the individual. And injustices do occur on this side of our legal tug-of-war as well as on the other side.

For example, in 1996, just a few weeks after the Turriago conviction was reversed, three Chicago men were finally released from prison after serving 18 years for a murder they didn't commit. The men, Verneal Jimerson, Dennis Williams, and Kenny Adams, had been arrested and convicted in 1978; a fourth man, Willie

Raines, had been convicted of the crime in 1984. This man, too, had been cleared and released a few weeks before the three other men. "The police just picked up the first four young black men they could, and that was it. They didn't care if we were guilty or innocent," said Dennis Williams, who spent most of his prison time on death row and now works to help others who have been wrongly convicted.

Mistakes do happen within our legal system. That fact is undeniable. And yet for all its flaws, the American legal system is still better than many systems that exist in other parts of the world. In many nations the courts are corrupt, controlled by the government, and citizens have no guarantee to a fair and just trial. The question is not whether we should remake our legal system altogether, but rather how we can best enforce our laws so that individual citizens can live their lives in safety.

Throughout this book, reference has frequently been made to the tug-of-war between public security and individual rights. But just what does the term "public security" imply? What kind of safety does a government need to offer its citizens? After all, the "public" is made up of individuals. Is the conflict between individual freedom and public safety real or an illusion?

In fact, perhaps the differences between the two sides of our tug-of-war are not as insurmountable as we might suppose. In reality they may be the two sides of one coin. The individuals who make up society need to be secure in the notion that they can reside in their homes without being rousted and mistreated by police. By the same token, each individual needs to be secure in the fact that if a crime does occur, law enforcement officials will use all the resources at hand in order to help victims obtain justice and restitution. The individuals who make up the public body also need to be secure in the fact that constitutional procedures apply to everyone, so that the truly innocent will get the

"Equal Justice Under Law" reads the inscription across the front of the U.S. Supreme Court building in Washington, D.C. In its rulings, the Court strives to keep a balance between the need for police to work effectively and the rights of all American citizens to be protected from overzealous prosecution.

opportunity for a level playing field and will be able to present their case protected by procedural law. When critics accuse our legal system of protecting the rights of the criminal, perhaps they miss the fact that those are each and every citizen's rights as well. The defense attorney defends not just the criminal, but us all.

Obviously our courts still need to be vigilant against the injustices that do occur. But the good thing about the American legal system is that it is not cast in stone; as new cases are tried and appealed, as new precedents are set, our laws constantly grow, constantly adapt both to the changing needs of our world and to a growing vision of justice. Although the Constitution was written more than 200 years ago, the Supreme

Court has the power to interpret it according to the Court's developing understanding of the spirit of the Constitution. Some of the Supreme Court's interpretations have occasionally resulted in a complete reversal of an earlier ruling, and a few Supreme Court decisions have led to major changes in our society. This is because justice is seldom a black-and-white concept. It is a difficult concept to grasp, let alone enforce, but it is the ideal our courts pursue.

When the authors of the Constitution designed the law of our land, they put in place a system of checks and balances, to keep any one branch of the government from becoming too powerful. In other words, they set up a three-sided tug-of-war between the courts, the legislature, and the executive branch of the government. This tug-of-war is a good and healthy thing, because it protects the public from any branch of government becoming so powerful that it trespasses on the freedom of the individual.

In the same way, the legal tug-of-war between public security and the rights of the individual in the long run protects both society as a whole and the individual, too. The conflict between the two points of view is healthy, stimulating our legal system to work toward a balanced justice. After all, the rights of the accused belong to all of us. They help safeguard us all, as individuals and as a society.

Bibliography

Amar, Akhil Reed. *The Constitution and Criminal Procedure: First Principles*. New Haven, Conn.: Yale University Press, 1997.

Belli, Melvin M., Sr., and Allen P. Wilkinson. *Everybody's Guide to the Law*. San Diego: Harcourt Brace Jovanovich, 1986.

Chambers, Mortimer, et al., eds. *The Western Experience: To the Eighteenth Century*. New York: McGraw-Hill, 1995.

Dix, George E., and M. Michael Sharlot. *Basic Criminal Law: Cases and Materials*. St. Paul, Minn.: West Publishing, 1987.

Henson, Burt M., and Ross R. Olney. *Furman v. Georgia: The Death Penalty and the Constitution*. New York: Franklin Watts, 1996.

Kamisar, Yale, Wayne R. LaFave, and Jerold H. Israel. *Basic Criminal Procedure*. St. Paul, Minn.: West Publishing, 1994.

Leinwand, Gerald. *Do We Need a New Constitution?* New York: Franklin Watts, 1994.

Maguire, Mike, Rod Morgan, and Robert Reiner, eds. *The Oxford Handbook of Criminology*. New York: Oxford University Press, 1997.

Roleff, Tamara L., ed. *The Legal System: Opposing Viewpoints*. San Diego: Greenhaven Press, 1996.

Saeger, Michael. *Defend Yourself Against Criminal Charges*. Naperville, Ill.: Sourcebooks, 1997.

Schmidt, Steffen W., Mack C. Shelley II, and Barbara A. Bardes. *American Government and Politics Today*. Belmont, Calif.: Wadsworth, 1997.

Territo, Leonard, James B. Halsted, and Max L. Bromley. *Crime and Justice in America: A Human Perspective*. St. Paul, Minn.: West Publishing, 1995.

Wice, Paul B. *Gideon v. Wainwright and the Right to Counsel*. New York: Franklin Watts, 1995.

———. *Miranda v. Arizona*. New York: Franklin Watts, 1996.

Index

Index

Index

Picture Credits

ANDREA CAMPBELL, a diplomate and fellow of the American College of Forensic Examiners, holds a degree in Criminal Justice and does forensic reconstruction sculpture for law enforcement. She has written several books, articles for a variety of educational magazines, and a weekly newspaper column. She lives in Hot Springs Village, Arkansas, with her husband, Michael.

AUSTIN SARAT is William Nelson Cromwell Professor of Jurisprudence and Political Science at Amherst College, where he also chairs the Department of Law, Jurisprudence and Social Thought. Professor Sarat is the author or editor of 23 books and numerous scholarly articles. Among his books are *Law's Violence, Sitting in Judgment: Sentencing the White Collar Criminal,* and *Justice and Injustice in Law and Legal Theory.* He has received many academic awards and held several prestigious fellowships. He is President of the Law & Society Association and Chair of the Working Group on Law, Culture and the Humanities. In addition, he is a nationally recognized teacher and educator whose teaching has been featured in the *New York Times,* on the *Today* show, and on National Public Radio's *Fresh Air.*